ISBN 978-1-331-14243-0
PIBN 10149914

This book is a reproduction of an important historical work. Forgotten Books uses
state-of-the-art technology to digitally reconstruct the work, preserving the original format
whilst repairing imperfections present in the aged copy. In rare cases, an imperfection in
the original, such as a blemish or missing page, may be replicated in our edition. We do,
however, repair the vast majority of imperfections successfully; any imperfections that
remain are intentionally left to preserve the state of such historical works.

1 MONTH OF
FREE
READING

at

www.ForgottenBooks.com

By purchasing this book you are eligible for one month membership to ForgottenBooks.com, giving you unlimited access to our entire collection of over 700,000 titles via our web site and mobile apps.

To claim your free month visit: www.forgottenbooks.com/free149914

English
Français
Deutsche
Italiano
Español
Português

www.forgottenbooks.com

Mythology Photography **Fiction**
Fishing Christianity **Art** Cooking
Essays Buddhism Freemasonry
Medicine **Biology** Music **Ancient**
Egypt Evolution Carpentry Physics
Dance Geology **Mathematics** Fitness
Shakespeare **Folklore** Yoga Marketing
Confidence Immortality Biographies
Poetry **Psychology** Witchcraft
Electronics Chemistry History **Law**
Accounting **Philosophy** Anthropology
Alchemy Drama Quantum Mechanics
Atheism Sexual Health **Ancient History**
Entrepreneurship Languages Sport
Paleontology Needlework Islam
Metaphysics Investment Archaeology
Parenting Statistics Criminology
Motivational

The world seemed laid out like a great race-course . and ▓▓▓▓ reach the runners trampled over the bodies goal. I saw that T

THREE DREAMS

BY

HUGH BLACK

FLEMING H. REVELL COMPANY

NEW YORK · CHICAGO · TORONTO

LONDON   EDINBURGH

82016B

THE · PLIMPTON · PRESS
[W · D · O]
NORWOOD · MASS · U · S · A

THREE DREAMS

THREE
DREAMS

THERE are times when we live as
in a dream, when the whole world is
other than it seems. The dreamer of
dreams lives in another world. He
walks in a beautiful light that never
was on sea or land, and the glory is
over all. In the hearts of many
around us there is such joy of the
dream that they can hardly keep
from laughter and singing — a dream
of beauty and peace and love that
changes the world and illumines all
life.

Some live in it all their days.
They walk in the light, and seem

never to know that there is darkness at all. They see beauty, and are compassed about by love. They see God in the world and feel Him in their hearts, and live as simply and naturally as the lilies and the birds. Others wake out of the dream disillusioned, and know what darkness and despair are, and how bitter is the death of a dream.

Happy to live in Beulah Land all the years; and happy even to see once the Delectable Mountains far off. Blessed to grow up in the Kingdom and never stray from its bounds; and blessed even to see the Kingdom once.

In my dream I saw that the world was fair, that beauty was all around, that the human verdict on creation as well as the divine verdict was that it is very good. The whole universe chanted a pæan of praise, the stars in their courses sang aloud for joy, the hills danced, and the trees clapped their hands. Praise went up like incense, and there was not a discord in the whole harmony. The earth praised God in every fiber of it and every power, even the dragons and the deeps — fire and hail, snow and vapors, stormy wind fulfilling His word, mountains and hills, fruit-ful trees and cedars, beasts and cat-tle, creeping things and flying fowl. The sun and the moon praised him, and the stars of light, and the heaven of heavens, and all that is above the heavens.

I saw the earth clothed with praise as with a garment. And I said, I too will extol thee, my God O King, and I will praise Thy name for ever and ever. Great is the Lord and greatly to be praised, and His greatness is unsearchable. One generation shall praise Thy works to another, and shall declare Thy mighty acts. They shall speak of the glory of Thy Kingdom and talk of Thy power, to make known to the sons of men the mighty acts and the glorious majesty of Thy Kingdom. I saw in my dream that it was so. The world of men praised the God of the living, as the world of nature praised the God of the dead.

I saw the militant Church as a great army terrible with banners

coming home after its bloodless vic-
tories, and on every banner gleamed
the triumphant cross, that had drawn
all men to it. Every eye that saw the
sacred symbol glowed with joy, and
every knee was bent, and every tongue
confessed that Jesus Christ is Lord to
the glory of God the Father. And the
nations of the earth repented them of
their sins of hatred and strife. They
turned their swords into ploughshares
and their spears into pruning-hooks,
and they followed war no more.

I saw kings and princes and rulers
cast down their crowns and scepters
before the conquering Christ. He
had come to His own, and His own
at last had received him. Men took
back the symbols of their place and
power at His hands, humbly to serve
Him and praise Him with their gentle
and generous deeds.

I saw the rich bring their wealth to His feet, pouring out their treasures, and they took it back from His hands, sanctified and purified, to be used in His service. I learned that the service of the Son of Man was the service of men. All who had power, or position, or wealth, or gifts of brain or hand, had learned the same lesson.

I saw the poor, truly poor in spirit, without envy or jealousy or malice, praising the King in their hearts, serving the Master in their work. There was no strife nor fear nor discord; for love reigned supreme. The cross had conquered and was in every heart, and the knowledge of the love of God, with its attesting fact of the love of men, covered the whole earth as the waters cover the sea.

I saw that the city — the city of my love — was as the city of God, with its towers and minarets gleaming in the radiance like the stainless peaks of the Alps. The shame of the city had been swallowed up, and the sin of it had become holiness, and the sorrow of it had disappeared. The streets of the city were full of boys and girls playing in the streets thereof. The work of the fathers was praise, and the play of the children was praise. The homes of the city, the city of my love now the city of God, were beautiful with love and peace and sweet content — Christian homes where children were taught by example the wondrous love of God. The cross was everywhere. It gleamed high over the streets on the domes and towers of the churches. It dominated all the houses of the people, and most of all, it left its mark on every heart.

I saw that it was so over all the world, not only in the city of my love. Nation vied with nation to right all wrongs and relieve all oppressed. Man emulated man in loving service. And the meek inherited the earth. It had come true at last, the dream of the dreamers, the vision of the seers, the hope of the prophets, the fulfilment of the Christ.

I saw in my dream that there was joy in heaven, and I beheld and lo! a great multitude which no man could number, clothed with white robes, and palms in their hands, saying, Blessing and glory and thanksgiving and honor and power and might be unto our God for ever and ever. And I said Amen.

What are these which are arrayed

in white robes? and whence came they? And I heard for answer, These are they which serve God day and night, and they hunger no more, neither thirst any more, and God has wiped away all tears from their eyes. And I heard as it were the voice of a great multitude, and as the voice of many waters, and as the voice of many thunderings, saying, Alleluia, for the Lord God omnipotent reigneth. Let us be glad and rejoice and give honor to Him. And I was glad with a great gladness that thrilled through all my being and awoke me from my dream.

I awoke and behold it was a dream. O God, *it was only a dream!*

II

Again I seemed to see in a dream, this time uncolored by the wish to see anything but the very truth, only the truth as it is and things as they are.

I saw things as they are, in their naked reality. I saw the world without any disguise, and life without a mask. The clear cold light of truth seemed to scatter the films of fancy from my eyes. I saw that the material was everything and there was nothing else, no reality but the outside, no meaning but the immediate and the evident, no purpose but the causal, no God but force. The heaven seemed to narrow itself down to the horizon, and there was nothing beyond. It must have been a dream; it was too clear-cut and certain for physical vision.

In my dream I saw that men lived out this God-less creed, or want of creed. Self dominated life. The cross was displanted and dethroned. The lust of the flesh drove men in blind passion; the lust of the eye lured them unresisting: the pride of life directed their course. Man was in the toils of forces without pity or remorse. Man distrusted man, and nation feared nation. The generous instincts died out of princely hearts; for it was accepted that the only rule for a sane life was that every man should be for himself. Oppression lifted up its head, and jealousy and envy and fear kept even the well-disposed from inter-fering. Magnanimity was sneered on as foolish knight-errantry. No nation could be generous and risk anything for the right.

I saw that class was raised against class in bitter strife. The rich clutched their riches the more closely: the poor thrust out envious hands to snatch their portion. Some devil's axioms had taken hold of the minds of men, that competition was the rule of life, that the weakest must go to the wall.

I saw that it was so. For the world seemed laid out like a great race-course, broad at the start and narrowing more and more so that fewer and fewer could run abreast, and the course was strewn with the failures and those crushed to the wall, and other eager runners trampled over their bodies to reach the goal.

Worst of all, I saw that *there was no goal.* The motto of the race was: every man for himself and the devil take the hindmost. And I saw that the devil could keep pace with the swiftest, and took not the hindmost but the foremost, for as the foremost reached what seemed the goal, he was dragged down somewhere and I saw him no more. It was too terrible, and I felt it must be a dream.

In the terror of it I said, Where is Christ? Has He done nothing of what I had dreamed before? Poor fool was I surely, living in a fool's paradise; where is the Christ of my dream? For answer I saw Him, the purest and the sweetest of the sons of men, I saw Him, a blighted blasted thing upon a cross, with heaven's lightnings playing in derision over His head, and the jeers of the crowd in His ears, "Let Him come down from the cross, if He be the King." A whisper of hope came to my heart,

He can; He will; let Him come down and convince the ribald crowd. But there was no answer. The cross stood dark against the twilight sky, and the earth shook with the pity of it all. And the veil of the temple was rent in twain and I saw behind it, and there was nothing — wood and stone and rags, the hocus-pocus of priests.

I found myself back in the city, the city of my love which I once fondly dreamed was the city of God, and it was night. The smoke of it went up to heaven, and it was as the smoke of hell. The streets flickered weirdly ghostlike in the flickering light. I knew all the time that it was a dream, and I was glad. I saw in my dream the sins of the streets. I saw into the houses, the haunts of misery and the dens of shame. I saw that there were in the city hells where human hearts wore themselves out in hopeless pain. I saw the rich fool choking his soul with gold, and the poor fool drowning his soul with drink. I saw children with the light of youth faded from their eyes, with sly crafty looks, some with gaunt wolfish cheeks, some with the iniquity of the fathers visited upon them to the third and fourth generations. I said, Thank God that it is only a dream, a hateful vision that shall pass.

I saw men so filled with the rage for gain that they forgot the rights of their fellows and the ideals of freedom. It seemed as if they were quenching the flame of the sacred torch and defacing liberty in the lust for gold. It seemed like another crucifixion.

I saw that there was no thought of God, no praise of Him in a city of churches. I heard women cursing men and yet living, and men cursing God and yet not able to die. I comforted myself with the thought that it was only a dream. I hugged the thought to my heart that when I awoke it would be all different. It was only a nightmare of the fancy. Until, above the tearless sob of mourners, the fearful sound of Rachel weeping for her children, above the giddy revelry of the gay, above the laughter and the music and the sound of dancing, above the curses and the pathetic make-belief of joy, through the night there came a woman's shriek, as if hell had outclimaxed itself at last, a piercing shriek of pain and despair that passed through ear and heart, bones and marrow like sharp steel, and it shivered through the air and lost itself in the God-less sky above. And I awoke with the agony of it.

I awoke and behold it was not a dream. O God of mercy and of pity, *it was no dream!*

III

Again I seemed to walk as in a vision and to see as in a dream. I was led back to the cross, and it stood clear against the sky. A hand touched my eyes, and I saw the pathos of it and the mystery of it and, most of all, the power of it. I saw the lightnings, that before seemed to play derisively above it, gather into a glory round the sacred head. I saw sad-eyed women and men and angels near it, but the sadness was swallowed up in love and adoration. Somehow I was drawn to it, as all men shall be drawn to it, and I said with gathering awe, It is the Master. And I fell upon my face and the mystery enveloped me and the glory blinded me, and like another doubting disciple I could only gasp out my repentance and confession, My Lord and my God.

In the light of the cross I looked upon all the world and upon all life. In the light of the cross I saw Satan fall from heaven like lightning. I saw the Kingdom of Heaven coming in like a resistless tide, never hasting, never resting, flooding the creeks and inlets. I saw through history a power making for righteousness, not by blind chance, but as part of a great design, part of a divine purpose, and I saw it to be a purpose of love, a purpose to redeem. I saw even the wrath of man working out the righteousness of God. I saw that the meek did inherit the earth, that the proud were brought down from their seat and those of low degree exalted.

I saw the world as the garment of

God, woven at the loom of time, a garment without seam like that of the blessed body of His Christ. And it was very good, with a deeper, richer, more mysterious beauty than before. The minor keys and the discords in the vocal score melted into the full harmony of the music of the spheres, and the discords were needed for the harmony.

I saw into the heart of the world, and it was the heart of God: I saw into the heart of God, and it was the heart of Christ: I saw into the heart of Christ, and it almost broke my heart when I saw the blood of His love, a divine, brooding, ineffable love. Round the cross as round the cradle there was the same circlet of praise — the old Christmas song, Glory to God in the highest and on earth peace, goodwill to men.

Back once more into the city, and I saw that it *was* the city of God, the scene of His redemptive work. I saw that amid the grossness and the slag there nestled the seed perfection, and the seed burst into a living thing, and it grew, and it had hope in its bosom. I saw the beauty of sacrifice in many a life, and even soiled characters glorified by an unselfish devotion, and love everywhere — love everywhere — bringing men to God. I saw men and women bending their necks meekly to hard yokes for love's sake, and humble duty ennobling many a life. I saw human love being redeemed from passion by pain, and gold coming from the furnace purified by fire, and sin being washed away by blood. In the light of the cross I saw that all things, of joy and sorrow, of gain and loss, of life and death, work together for good to them that love the Lord.

Was this too a dream? If so, it was a deeper and a larger one than the first. It at least was not a blinding of the eyes to facts, not a whispering of peace when there was no peace, not a pretense that there was no pain and sorrow and sin and death. But it saw these things, and yet saw them to have a meaning, to be part of the program, not an unrehearsed accident but part of the purpose of the great World-Artist. And I beheld and lo! a great multitude stood before the Lamb, clothed with white robes, and I said, What are these which are arrayed in white robes? and whence came they? These are they which came out of the great tribulation.

I saw some of these saints in their

tribulation in the city, and they made the city the city of God. When I saw them I seemed to see the Master Himself, giving Himself for the world anew, saving it by love, redeeming it by blood. I saw Him seeking the lost, making hearts rise with a new hope, making eyes shine with a new light. And I follow Him that I may but touch the hem of His garment.

Is it a dream, this vision of the Christ and the power of His cross and the beauty of His love? Is it a dream that the promise of Christmas is being fulfilled? Are we deluding ourselves when we keep the birthday of the Prince of Peace?

Is it a dream? Nay, but the lack of it a dream
And failing it, life's lore and wealth a dream.
And all the world a dream.

Is it a dream that He comes stilling the wild tempest of human passion, creating His eternal brotherhood, establishing His Kingdom of righteousness and peace and love and joy, lifting the world in its steep ascent to God?

From that dream I have not yet awakened, and I pray God I may never awake.